MEMORIES OF THE 1950's – 1960's

No. 38 SOUTH & WEST YORKS

KEITH PIRT DON BEECROFT & RON HODGE

C000278224

Copyright Book Law Publications 2012
ISBN 978-1-907094-86-6

INTRODUCTION

To say that Yorkshire's railway system was interesting would be an understatement. Likewise, diverse seems hardly adequate to describe the variety of routes, pre-Grouping infrastructure, rolling stock, motive power, etc., etc. In a nutshell, Yorkshire's railways were magical. Everything and anything was available for those who wanted either the everyday or the different. Industry, countryside, urban, rural, quiet, manic. You name it, Yorkshire had it. Nowadays, it is very different! However, we are focussing on the Fifties' and Sixties', the final decades of the period when the railways were at their zenith, when the summit of expansion had been attained and contraction (coined as rationalisation at the time) began its slow strangulation of what we, perhaps, regarded as normal.

Hopefully, the images contained within will help readers remember those times when Yorkshire's railway system was – interesting! We have purposely only covered what was once known as the West Riding and, chosen the title 'South and West Yorkshire' to add some modernism. There will probably be other titles in this series covering further areas of England's largest county – North, East, and perhaps more on the south, or even west! It was a big place, and interesting!

Cover picture: **MSW EM1 No.26005 and an unidentified sister enter Penistone in July 1955 with a long train of mineral empties for Wath yard.** *K.R.Pirt.*

Previous page: **Class 4 No.42238 lifts the 10.5 a.m. Bradford (Exchange) – Paignton through the junction at St Dunstans on 27th May 1967.** *Ron Hodge.*

Printed and bound by The Amadeus Press, Cleckheaton, West Yorkshire
First published in the United Kingdom by Book Law Publications, 382 Carlton Hill, Nottingham, NG4 1JA

We start off our journey through south and west Yorkshire at our most northerly point – Starbeck engine shed near Harrogate. We don't have an exact date for this illustration but Q6 No.63436 is sporting a 50B Neville Hill shed plate and the 0-8-0 was allocated to that depot from 25th January 1953 and 16th June 1957, and again from December 1959 but that latter date can be discounted because behind the Q6 is New England V2 No.60897 which is wearing a 35A shedplate, New England's code until changed to 34E in July 1958! Therefore, take your pick for anytime between January 1953 and June 1957. You will note that dates become much more precise as we progress on out journey southwards to Sheffield. Finally, note the ancient six-wheel breakdown van on the right which now carries the legend 'Motive Power Depot', and 'Starbeck' on different planks whilst in between the two is the painted-out LNER usage 'Loco Dept.' *David Dalton.*

3

With eleven vehicles behind the locomotive, the 10.00 a.m. Bradford (Forster Square)–Paignton (1V39), also known as *THE DEVONIA*, departs from the Bradford terminus behind Holbeck 'Peak' D35 on Saturday 25th March 1967. The location of this former Midland Railway passenger station on the northern fringe of the city centre meant that all departures headed northwards at least as far as Shipley before they could change direction, no matter which way they were heading. It's nice to see the long snaking train threading its way past the yards as the big diesel slowly accelerates in a northbound direction. The numerous junctions and curves encountered by this train during the first dozen miles or so of its journey meant that D35 would not be able to show its paces but then the train soon had to terminate at Leeds (City) prior to reversing with another Type 4 taking the train on its southward journey. This particular working had numerous stops on its way to Devon, likewise crews would change frequently but the same locomotive would take the formation all the way to the 'English Riviera' and then work back to Leeds the following day with the northbound train. Forster Square station was opened in 1890, replacing an earlier establishment dating from 1846 known as Market Street. The station still serves Bradford today, albeit almost a quarter mile further north from its original location. It was re-located in 1990 and comprises two long platforms which cater for Inter-City services whilst a third, shorter, platform is used for local traffic. The whole lot was electrified in 1994 as part of the Aire Valley electrification scheme. Pedestrian entrances consist a staircase from Cheapside and a footway from Forster Square business park. *Ron Hodge.*

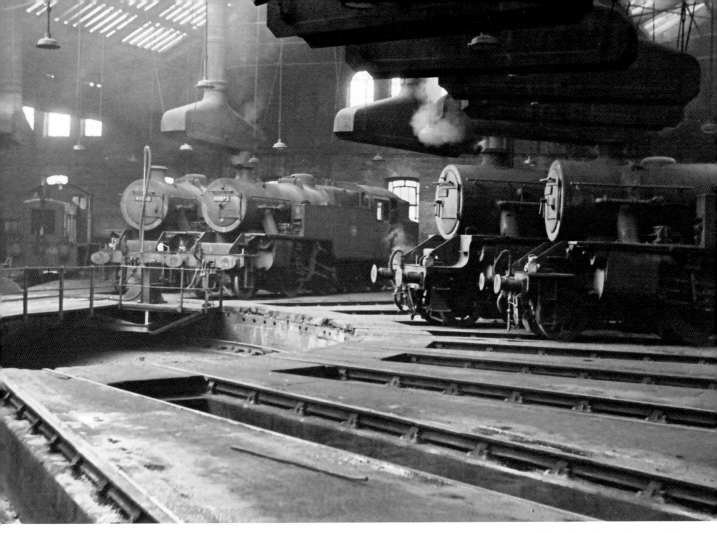

Shortly after leaving Forster Square behind, the observant passenger on that 10.00 a.m. departure would notice the engine shed at Manningham on the east side of the line, adjacent to the station of the same name. Being a former Midland shed, most of the engines would have been hidden from view inside the roundhouse anyway, and on Thursday 27th April 1967 the bulk of what was left of Manningham's allocation were doing just that with the ample accommodation of old now appearing rather extravagant in the circumstances. From a high of nearly fifty engines at the formation of British Railways, the depot was by now housing less than a dozen locomotives, all ex-LMS and BR Standard types. Besides the unidentified Drewry diesel-mechanical shunter, which could have been either of two shedded at Manningham during that last week of steam operation – D2044 or D2102, the four steam locomotives, from left to right, were: 42052, 42093, 44912 and 42138. Surprisingly the floor appears relatively tidy; perhaps the lack of residents has something to do with that. Manningham was opened in 1872 and it closed just three days after this scene was captured on film. *Ron Hodge.*

With a mixed and hefty looking parcels train in tow, 'Jubilee' No.45697 ACHILLES takes the Bradford route at Shipley Leeds junction on 29th April 1967. *Ron Hodge.*

Healey Mills based English Electric Type 4 D395 brings the Down *WAVERLEY* towards Leeds junction, Shipley on the glorious afternoon of Saturday 8th July 1967. During the period when it was departing from Forster Square, the southbound *DEVONIAN* would have passed from left to right on the first stage of its journey from Bradford. On the extreme right is the start of the branch line to Idle which is featured in the following illustration. *Ron Hodge.*

On 10th June 1967 the Bradford Valley Goods – Idle pick-up was in the charge of BR Sulzer Type 2 D5256. The diesels were fairly new to this steeply graded branch having taken over from steam which was taken off the line during the final week of the previous April (Manningham shed closed on the 30th). The branch was not looking its best at this time and only catered for this particular working which ceased in October 1968 when the branch was finally closed. Until the end of October 1964 through freights used this line but like much of the BR system at that period, the traffic dried up! Opened in 1875, the branch had a regular passenger service to Shipley (Windhill) up to 2nd February 1931; the trains also catered for the three intermediate stations along its length: Thackley, Idle and Eccleshill. However, the world-wide economic downturn of the period saw the stations closed as the LNER made savings wherever it could. Thereafter excursion traffic saw that the unstaffed but still intact stations got occasional use until the first section of the branch, that between Laisterdyke and Idle, was totally closed in October 1964. Today that circular stretch of railway skirting around the eastern suburbs of Bradford would perhaps make an ideal commuting route. *Ron Hodge.*

Back on the main line at Shipley, 'Jubilee' No.45675 runs towards Leeds with the 11.10 a.m. parcels train from Heysham on 29th April 1967. *Ron Hodge.*

On the south side of Bradford city centre was Exchange station which had its origins stretching back to 1850, when the Lancashire & Yorkshire Railway began to flex its muscles around the West Riding. In January 1867 the Great Northern Railway abandoned their terminus at Adolphus Street in favour of a joint station with the L&Y. That marriage lasted until Grouping when the LMS and LNER confirmed the arrangement which continued until BR brought everything under one umbrella. This view of Exchange throat on 17th June 1967 reveals Fairburn Cl.4 tank No.42073 departing from the terminus with the 5.20 p.m. Bradford (Exchange) to London (King's Cross). The 2-6-4T would have worked the train to Wakefield (Westgate) where the formation would be combined with a service from Leeds and taken on to King's Cross by a Type 4 or perhaps a Type 5 diesel locomotive. The massive retaining walls here are an indication of the huge construction requirements employed to keep the inclination of the railway to a reasonable and workable degree as it approached the terminus. As it worked out, the slope from north to south still rises at roughly 1 in 50 from the platform ends. The exhaust displayed by the Cl.4 tank is evidence of the sudden climb and gravity combining to make it a difficult location to depart from with a trailing load. *Ron Hodge.*

otplatemen pass the time of day at Bradford (Exchange) on 20th May 1967 as Cl.4 No.42235 tries to remain anonymous on platform 8 ter bringing in empty stock from Low Moor carriage sidings. The time is approximately 8.30 a.m. on what appears to be a bright sunny turday morning. Besides the newly arrived stock, one of the vehicles from *THE YORKSHIRE PULLMAN* (Bradford portion) hides hind the Fairburn tank alongside platform 9, whilst on the right at platform 7 a Metro-Camm diesel unit awaits departure time. Within years this station, as part of the inner city renewal project for Bradford, was to be relocated some 200 yards further south on part of e site once occupied by Bridge Street goods depot. Some ten years later, in 1983, when all the components for road transport section of e scheme were in place, the station lost some of its former identity when it became simply Bradford Interchange. *Ron Hodge.*

The uninspiring cladding covering the gables of the train sheds at Exchange did little to enhance the neglected appearance of th[e] Bradford terminus. On Saturday 24th June 1967 Cl.4 No.42689 stands at the head of the Paignton train, *THE DEVONIAN*, in platfor[m] 10 waiting as the 10.00 a.m. departure time approaches. The yard to the right was known as Vicar Lane goods, ex-GNR, and was used f[or] short-term stabling of carriage stock in 1967. *Ron Hodge.*

The Normanton-Bradford parcels train has just arrived at the throat of Exchange station on 10th June 1967 behind Cl.4 No.42138. An inspection of the undergear appears to be taking place whilst the guard looks out. The vehicle, I am reliably informed, is one of the numerous LMS built (Period III 50ft BG) Full Brake, with a ducket and now probably dedicated solely to parcels workings. On the adjacent track 'Jubilee' No.45697 ACHILLES heads a private excursion (1Z13) destined for Blackpool. By now the 'Jubilee' class is down to just a few members, all based in this area, 45697 was allocated to Holbeck at this time but not for much longer as by September it would be withdrawn as North Eastern Region steam was banished to oblivion! Note the weed strewn yard of the erstwhile Lancashire & Yorkshire Railway Bridge Street goods depot. The whole establishment appears to be waiting patiently for demolition prior to redevelopment of its prime location right in the centre of town. The place had already been closed for nearly five years but it would be another five before the site was used for the Bradford transport interchange. *Ron Hodge.*

A little later on that morning of 10th June, at Mill Lane/St Dunstans, the aforementioned 'Jubilee' lifts its train out of Bradford but being usurped by Cl.4 tank No.42073 which is taking the former GNR route with the Bradford (Exchange) – Paington. The ruling gradie of 1 in 50 out of Exchange was always guaranteed to produce plenty of exhaust from the steam locomotives involved. The Blackpo train engine would have to continue working hard nearly all the way to Low Moor whereas the tank engine would find its route through Dunstans and Hammerton Street a little easier in comparison. *Ron Hodge.*

Even with banking assistance from a 2-6-4T, No.45697 (note the lack of nameplate) is making heavy weather of the climb past Mill Lane. The external condition of the engine leaves a lot to be desired compared with some of the other Holbeck 'Jubilees' at this time such as No.45562 and 45675 which always appeared immaculate and were favourites for railtours. *Ron Hodge.*

Approaching the Mill Lane/St Dunstans junction on Saturday 27th May 1967, Low Moor Cl.4 No.42235 has charge of the 9.12 a.m. Bradford (Exchange) – St Pancras express which it would work as far as Leeds (City). *Ron Hodge.*

Taking it nice and steady as it passes Mill Lane signal box, Cl.4 No.42251 works 3Z55 empty carriage stock from Low Moor into Exchange station on Tuesday 30th May 1967. The two lines going off to the left of the picture consist the former Great Northern trackage through St Dunstans and the route to Halifax and Keighley. This whole area, like most large city termini approaches, was festooned with goods yards, coal yards, carriage sidings, and junctions. *Ron Hodge.*

Seen from the Down platform of the erstwhile St Dunstans station, Holbeck Cl.4 No.42689 runs into Mill Lane junction with its train still on St Dunstans junction on the evening of 7th July 1967. The three-coach formation is the remains of the northbound *DEVONIAN*. The two lines going off to the left beneath the last carriage, was the former GNR route to Halifax and Keighley. On the right are the remains of St Dunstans station Up platform which became redundant some fifteen years earlier in September 1952. The station was created in 1878 on a triangular layout to serve both the Leeds and the Halifax lines. *Ron Hodge.*

The Halifax line platforms of St Dunstans station on 7th July 1967 with Cl.4 No.42689 now propelling its three-coach train towards the carriage siding at St Dunstans which can be seen on the right. The manoeuvre would take the tank and its formation beneath the L&Y main line, so that it could set back into the sidings, uncouple, and exit the yard light. The road bridge spanning the Low Moor line in the distance was Ripley Street bridge from which some of the illustration in this section of the album were captured on film. The wooden building on the left, which was adjacent to the signal box, was still in use and even has a broom propped against the wall. *Ron Hodge.*

A fine view of the St Dunstans/Mill Lane junction layout as Cl.4 No.42073 eases around the curve with the 5.20 p.m. Bradford (Exchange)–King's Cross on 5th July 1967. Although foliage has obscured much of the station remains, the signal box stands out in its new coat of paint which marked its operational status. Beyond the main line to Low Moor and partly hidden by the Up signal for the GN lines, Mill Lane signal box can just be made out in the afternoon shadows. *Ron Hodge.*

he view northwards from Ripley Street bridge revealed this vista of the main line to Low Moor with Cl.4 No.42616 hauling empty arriage stock up the incline to Low Moor carriage sidings on Saturday 8th July 1967. At the rear of the formation a 'Peak' diesel, which ad brought the train from Cleethorpes to Bradford, is perhaps helping out with the nine-coach train. The ensemble is about to cross the ridge over the ex-GN line to Halifax and Keighley, via the Queensbury triangle, which swung round from St Dunstans before heading ff in a westerly direction. That line lost its passenger service in 1955, the section from Queensbury to Keighley closed altogether. The alifax High Level line through Holmfield remained open for goods trains until June 1960. The only traffic over this section of the railway n 1967 was the goods to traffic to City Road goods yard and the e.c.s. workings to St Dunstans carriage sidings visible just above the tank ocomotive. On the left of the main line, opposite the rear portion of the train is the closed Springmill Street coal yard. *Ron Hodge.*

Bursting into the cutting on the eastern side of the St Dunstans triangle, Cl.4 No.42066 brings the 10.00 a.m. Bradford (Exchange)–Paignton *THE DEVONIAN* through the curve on a glorious 1st July 1967. Note that although the train has moved from Forster Square terminus to Exchange, the original departure time has at least been preserved. *Ron Hodge.*

Looking more like an expansive model railway layout than a typical piece of BR real estate from the end of the steam era, this view at Laisterdyke shows BR Sulzer Type 2 D5100 – deputising for a Cl.4 tank! – working a Bradford (Exchange)–King's Cross express on 20th May 1967. *Ron Hodge.*

Brush Type 4 D1108 seems hardly taxed as it passes through Laisterdyke with the King's Cross–Bradford (Exchange) on 16th May 196? Again, lots of railway infrastructure is evident but not for much longer as BR started to tighten its belt with rationalisation and the sellin of land throughout the county. *Ron Hodge.*

Seen from the Down island platform of the closed Laisterdyke station, the 7.15 a.m. Bradford (Exchange)–King's Cross accelerates away from Laisterdyke West Junction on a damp 30th May 1967. Although perfectly safe and having stood for decades, the ex-GNR cantilevered signal box still had a somewhat precarious demeanour about its existence. On the left, at platform end, the LNER trespass notice – some nineteen years after that company ceased to exist – still warns of the financial penalties suffered by unauthorised persons going beyond that point. The station had closed on 4th July 1966 some one hundred and twelve years after the original station was opened by the Great Northern. *Ron Hodge.*

Cl.4 No.42616 heads through Laisterdyke towards Bradford (Exchange) with the four-coach Bradford portion of the 1.45 p.m. express from King's Cross on Saturday 8th July 1967. *Ron Hodge.*

mmingham B1 No.61168 gets ready for the off with a mid-afternoon Cleethorpes train from platform 5 at Leeds (Central) on Saturday 4th April 1962. Alongside, and stabled on the middle road between platforms 4 and 5, is a Haymarket based 'Deltic' – D9004 – which has vorked into Central on the Up *QUEEN OF SCOTS* and is now awaiting the arrival of the Down service from King's Cross which it would ake forward to Glasgow via Harrogate and Northallerton. *David Dalton.*

On that same April afternoon in 1962, shortly after the departure of the Cleethorpes train and just as the sun comes out, the very best in ECML express motive power is brought together at Leeds (Central) in the shape of Copley Hill based Peppercorn A1 No.60115, which is making a big exhaust for a light engine movement. The Pacific has just been released after bringing in the empty stock of the Cleethorpes train featured in the previous illustration. As it runs out of platform 5 it will take up a position to await the arrival of its own carriage stock for the Up working of *THE WHITE ROSE* to King's Cross. *David Dalton.*

The introduction of diesel multiple units on the Bradford (Exchange)–Leeds (Central) route in June 1954 saw a rise in passenger numbers using the services compared with the steam hauled trains which they replaced. The subsequent problems experienced by the diesel units shortly afterwards, concerning the torque converters, has been well documented previously so there is no need to linger on that point. However, BR did eventually prevail and a wide ranging suburban network was soon covered by these multiple units in West Yorkshire. One of the 'guilty' units – a Derby Lightweight two-car formation with motor composite E79500 leading, E79000 trailing – is featured here entering platform 6 at Leeds (Central) on a service from Bradford (Exchange) to Knaresborough on 22nd May 1955. *Ron Hodge.*

Long before Huddersfield Hillhouse engine shed became part of the North Eastern Region its shed code was 25B under Wakefield 25A. In September 1956 the Wakefield district sheds, minus Huddersfield, were transferred the NER control leaving 25B out on its own until the following February when Hillhouse became 55G under the control of Holbeck. Effectively bringing the former London & North Western sheds under the same district as the ex-Midland sheds within the new NER boundary whilst the former Lancashire & Yorkshire depots were all now under Wakefield 56 district control. However, few of these regional boundary changes significantly altered traffic patterns. One duty undertaken by Hillhouse shed since pre-Grouping days was the nightly fitted goods train to Camden goods in London, a working for which the depot supplied motive power virtually up to closure in January 1967. On Sunday 21st March 1954 a rather small looking, actually ex-works, Stanier Class 5, No.45027 of Willesden shed, was to be the engine of that particular night's working which took the train over the Pennines through Standedge to Heaton Norris where the ex-LNWR main line from Manchester to the south was gained. At the London end a Huddersfield engine which had spent the weekend on shed at Willesden would then make its way home with the return working from Camden. *K.R.Pirt.*

Another of the former Lancashire & Yorkshire engine sheds affected by the regional boundary changes of September 1956 was Sowerby Bridge which became 56E from 25E. The allocation of 56E reflected its pre-Grouping ownership for much of the British Railways period with more than half the strength at Nationalisation made up of ex-L&Y locomotives. This Aspinall 2P 2-4-2T No.50757, seen stabled at the depot whilst acting as shed pilot on Sunday 21st March 1954, was a relative newcomer to the allocation having transferred from Newton Heath eleven months previously; within a few weeks of this photograph being taken it was on the move again when it re-allocated to Low Moor. Note the shed plate is still 25E. By 1950 the L&Y flavour was still strong at the shed with half of the allocation being ex-Business Line engines. However, during the next decade the ranks were depleted somewhat and by the end of 1959 only four 'A' class 0-6-0s represented the former owners of Sowerby Bridge engine shed. On the other hand the total allocation of locomotives had fallen by about a fifth. At closure in 1964 none of the ex-L&Y engines were around to see the event. Note the rather nice Pennine weather experienced during that March in 1954. *K.R.Pirt.*

You could be forgiven, after perusing this illustration, for thinking that Ardsley was a former Great Central engine shed with C14 No.6744[]
and an O4 2-8-0 present. It was however built by the Great Northern Railway in 1892. Nevertheless Ardsley was home to more that half o[]
the C14 class up to June 1951 when seven of the survivors were allocated. The last C14 s to leave this West Riding depot were Nos.6744[]
and 67446, which returned to Gorton in May 1955. This illustration indicates that the shed's northlight roof was showing serious sig[]
of neglect. Indeed the shed roof at this date, 2nd March 1952, was awaiting the second phase of a long overdue post-war rebuild whic[]
the eastern end of the shed had already partially received. The job was certainly long-winded but it was to be 1953 before the complet[]
rebuild was started at this end of the shed when the timber, slate and glass covering would eventually be replaced by one of the mor[]
32 robust precast concrete louvre type roofs favoured by the North Eastern Region at that period. *David Dalton.*

Two years later and on 21st March 1954 the motive power has changed little, but the shed itself has undergone massive changes. Still incomplete, the new roof supports are progressing with the walls prepared and concrete pads in position ready for the installation of the transverse pre-cast beams. By the end of the year the task would be finished and Ardsley could look forward to 11 years of uninterrupted operations up to closure. O4 No.63823 was a relative newcomer to 37A having transferred from Tuxford just four months previously. The O4 class became regular members of Ardsley's allocation shortly after Grouping and continued to serve the depot until the 1960s with ten of the class allocated for much of the BR period. *K.R.Pirt.*

With a long train of unfitted but empty mineral wagons in tow, WD No.90721 rattles the whole formation to a grinding halt whilst awaiting the signal on the through road at Wakefield (Kirkgate) station in August 1966. The WD 2-8-0 was synonymous with this area, Wakefield shed having one of the largest concentrations of the class in the country. This was coal country and the train depicted was destined for one of the local collieries; to say which one without the daily working timetable would be futile as there was so many in the district at this time with a myriad of trains serving them. Sadly, the collieries, like the WD class have all gone, their reserves, so we are told having been depleted. However, when this scene was captured coal traffic around Wakefield was still the main source of freight traffic income for BR and would remain so for some years, albeit in the hands of diesel locomotives. *D.H.Beecroft.*

There was obviously a line occupation issue here. Queuing up for the signal to take them to the shed, and seemingly whistling away to while away the time, York based EE Type 4 D396, complete with a brake tender, closely followed by an earlier member of the same class, stand on the through road at Wakefield (Kirkgate) on a sunny Saturday lunchtime in August 1966. By the end of the year D396 was chosen to become part of the allocation for the new depot at nearby Healey Mills yard and trips to Wakefield engine shed would become a thing of the past. *D.H.Beecroft.*

Another WD mineral working at Wakefield in August 1966 but this time its a loaded train probably bound for one of the coking plants Glasshoughton for instance; the contents of the wagons appearing to be of a quality suited to neither household or industrial use. Such was the intensity of the coal traffic through this station that trains going east or west could be empty or loaded, the traffic patterns being something of a puzzle to anyone other than those personnel involved in the workings. WD No.90465 was in fact a Normanton engine which would make Glasshoughton a favourite but not a definite destination! *D.H.Beecroft.*

This is WD No.90047 at the east end of Kirkgate station, waiting at the signal which always seemed to show a red aspect. A bit of damage to the cylinder covering does not detract from the usual WD turnout of filthy black. *D.H.Beecroft.*

This compiler makes no apology for the inclusion of four WD 2-8-0 illustrations; this was, after all, 'Dub-Dee' country! No.90404 ha[s] plenty in the boiler as it waits patiently for the signal which would take it to 56A at the end of its morning shift in August 1966. Except fo[r] just two weeks spent at Goole in February 1956, this engine spent the whole of its BR career allocated to Wakefield, being withdrawn a[t] the shed on 3rd June 1967. Some 150 WD 2-8-0s, more than a fifth of the class total, had been allocated to Wakefield shed at one time o[r] another, with fifty to sixty engines 'on the books' at any one time. So, we must leave Kirkgate station and look at some other aspects of th[e] railways in Yorkshire as we plod on in a southerly direction with deviations both west and east. *D.H.Beecroft.*

he afternoon sun of Sunday 11th November 1956 fights to brighten up a typical hazy winter day as A3 No.60058 runs past Wakefield shed th a diverted southbound express from Leeds to King's Cross. Showing a good exhaust to add to the already damp laden atmosphere, e Copley Hill based Pacific will not get too much of a chance to stretch its legs over the next thirty miles or so because this was mining untry with the ever present and constantly changing speed restrictions. *David Dalton.*

During its final months as a steam motive power depot, Wakefield played host to numerous classes. Besides the ubiquitous WD 2-8-0, B
Standard types were also allocated to 56A. Then came the many visitors from across the Pennines which turned up every day: Stanier Cla
5s, Cl.8F., and of course the Cl.9F 2-10-0s. If any class of steam locomotive could be said to have had a 'raw deal' it was the 9F. No.920
transferred to Wakefield in October 1966 from York. One of the original batch built for the Western Region in 1954, it was photograph
outside the southern end of Wakefield shed in March 1967, just a few weeks before withdrawal – just thirteen years old. Many would s
(that doesn't include the initially biased WR enginemen at Ebbw Junction shed) that the 2-10-0 was one of the best British locomotives ev
built. They certainly did what was expected of them and more besides; exploits hauling express passenger train on the East Coast ma
line and other routes, certainly endeared them to footplatemen, some operating authorities and enthusiasts alike but not to the powe
that-be who frowned upon the high speed running. If they had worked for the expected thirty-odd years, then who knows what the cla
might have achieved. No.92006 looks to be in fine fettle here, if a tad filthy, but it was actually unserviceable and would never work agai
Such was the dearth of withdrawn locomotives littering the former steam sheds in Yorkshire that it was some months before some of the
were sold for scrap. Our subject lingered at Wakefield for seven months before a scrap metal dealer from Hull purchased its hulk a
consigned it to oblivion! *D.H.Beecroft.*

This internal view of Wakefield engine shed on 20th March 1955 reveals one of the rapidly diminishing band of former Lancashire & Yorkshire Barton-Wright 2F 0-6-0s – No.52044. The only one of its kind still allocated to a ex-L&Y shed (No.52053, another 25A engine, had recently been condemned), 52044 would eventually be the only example of its class still active but in March 1955 Nos.52021 and 52051 were still working from Springs Branch in Wigan, whilst 52016 was active at Patricroft. The end of this ancient six-coupled locomotive took place in June 1959. Alongside is a miniature snowplough fitted WD 2-8-0, No.90607, the more usual fare found at Wakefield. In the background between the two locomotives can be glimpsed the shed's sheerlegs which unusually were inside the shed and required their own roof covering; an external view of the appliance can be made out in the illustration featuring the EE Type 3 passing the shed with a coal train. Note also the new roof set onto the old wall. *K.R.Pirt.*

English Electric Type 3 D6829 runs past Wakefield engine shed with a northbound coal train in June 1967. This type of working would normally have been the preserve of one of Wakefield's WD 2-8-0s but the remaining members of the once vast 56A allocation had all been withdrawn during that summer of 1967. Now, this Healey Mills based diesel, along with dozens of its sisters, has charge of the enormous mineral traffic still originating in the area. D6829 was delivered new to the Western Region at Cardiff Canton in March 1963 but with decreasing mineral traffic over the south Wales lines since that time, many of the EE Type 3s were drafted into the North Eastern Region to carry on where the WDs left off. Healey Mills depot, along with the adjacent marshalling yard, opened for business in June 1966 but it took a year before everything was entrusted to the diesel fleet allocated to that place. Though officially closed to steam, Wakefield engine shed was still operational with large numbers of diesels conveniently using the depot for stabling. A lot of steam locomotives were still resident on this date though they were 'dead' and awaiting sale to various scrap merchants. The structure housing the sheerlegs mentioned in a previous illustration can be seen in this view pointing skywards just above the centre of the range of northlight roofs atop the offices and stores. The coaling plant, now redundant too, stands defiantly after thirty-odd years serving Wakefield's steam fleet. *D.H.Beecroft.*

42

ewton Heath G3 class 'Austin Seven' No.49667 leads a northbound coal train through Oakenshaw towards Wakefield on a sunny Friday fternoon, 17th May 1956. Heading for Manchester, the 0-8-0 and its heavy load of household, gas works and industrial coal would e routed via Wakefield (Kirkgate), Horbury, Mirfield, Cooper Bridge, Elland, Sowerby Bridge, Todmorden, Littleborough, Middleton nction and then into one of the Manchester yards. Within a couple of years the population of the Fowler G3 class would have dwindled virtually nil and WD 2-8-0s would be doing most of the mineral train haulage over the former L&Y lines. *Ron Hodge.*

On the same afternoon Ron Hodge captured this scene from the same vantage point as the last picture but pointing the camera a littl further to the west. We see Crewe South 'Crab' No.42940 keeping a check of its reasonably heavy load of coal as it swings off the forme Midland main line at Oakenshaw South Junction and round the spur to the ex-L&Y line at Oakenshaw North Junction. The load appear to be made up entirely of industrial coal whilst the contents of the tender seem to be of a better quality. How this 5B engine got here i unknown but speculation would have seen it being serviced at Royston shed prior to heading home via Wakefield, Horbury, Mirfiel Huddersfield, Standedge, Stalybridge, Heaton Norris and Stockport. If any reader knows otherwise the compiler would like to know vi the publisher please. *Ron Hodge.*

With no sense of irony or insult intended with this illustration, we have Crewe-built 'Peak' D52 THE LANCASHIRE FUSILIER running through Royston & Notton station with an express to St Pancras in April 1967. This four platform station was opened in July 1900 replacing the 1841-built station which stood about a mile to the north of this site. This station too was closed, the lack of traffic seeing its demise on the first day of 1968. In the background the infrastructure of Yorkshire's one-time main industry, coal mining and processing, stands against the skyline above the residential housing, in the shape of Monckton Colliery and Coking plant. The all pervading aroma of the chemical conversion of coal into other products hanging over this area was a constant reminder of the processes being carried on round the clock, day in, day out, year after year, decade after decade. Alas it too has all now disappeared. *D.H.Beecroft.*

45

Just south of Royston & Notton station, on the east side of the line, the London Midland & Scottish Railway built a new locomotive dep which was opened for business in early 1932. The shed was built with Government aid in the shape of the Loans & Guarantees Act, incentive created in order to get the economy moving forwards after the global recession. Being in the virtual heart of the Yorkshi coalfield, and coal at that time being the lifeblood of British industry, it made sense to provide a locomotive depot whereby servici and turn-round time for freight locomotives was kept to a minimum therefore keeping the locomotives in traffic longer. The sh building itself consisted ten roads and was built to the most economical standards of the time but it was the layout of the depot whi was revolutionary in that no turntables had been provided (cost saving) and instead a triangle of lines had been laid around the shed that locomotives could be easily turned with the minimum of fuss. Also, a small mechanical coaling plant, working on a conveyor buck system, had been installed to speed up the laborious task of refilling empty tenders. This view of the depot on 12th March 1967 shows t usual allocation of numerous Stanier 8F freight engines along with a lone 'Jubilee' No.45562 ALBERTA. The 'namer' albeit not actua carrying its nameplates but sporting instead painted names on the backing plate, was visiting Royston shed for the weekend but how actually got there in the first place is unknown. Royston depot closed at the beginning of November 1967, its work done as the end of era came and went. Although diesels took over from steam working the coal trains, the new motive power did not require the intensi daily upkeep of steam therefore Royston shed became surplus to requirements. *Ron Hodge.*

undated, but certainly post March 1957, illustration of Royston allocated ex-Midland 1P 0-4-4T No.58066 seen from the Down platform
Barnsley (Court House) station. The 1P was used for a push-pull service which linked Barnsley with its nearest main line station at
dworth; the service itself being a throwback to Midland Railway days and gave a connection to London services. At a lower elevation,
d out of picture to the left, was the near adjacent Barnsley (Exchange) station which offered little more than a single platform but
vived to this day, albeit now with an addition platform, waiting room and footbridge, built after the engine shed was closed and
molished in January 1960. The little 0-4-4T did not last even that long, its final workings taking place prior to September 1958 when it
s condemned. One of the Royston based Ivatt Cl.2MT six-coupled tank engines with two non-corridor coaches worked the service from
reon until closure of the station. Court House station opened for business in May 1870, a joint venture between the Midland and Great
ntral. Note the sleeper/rail arrangement over the bridge alignment. *David Dalton.*

The view inside Barnsley (Court House), on that unknown date, when the 1P 0-4-4T No.58066 was waiting at the signal before proceedin
to Royston shed. Besides the demise of this engine, the introduction of diesel multiple units over the line through Barnsley (Exchange)
early 1958 added to the loss of the Court House-Cudworth services and the inevitable closure of Court House station. This view, capture
from a stationary multiple unit on the service from Sheffield (Midland), reveals modern electric fluorescent lighting – complete with th
station name on the covers – over the Up platform which must have been installed when the overall roof was replaced just a few yea
previously. The gradient post indicates a falling grade but has no other useful information! The station closed on the evening of Goo
Friday 16th April 1960 after the last train had departed at, apparently, 6.30 p.m. The d.m.u. service from Sheffield (Midland) was switch
to Barnsley (Exchange); earlier re-arrangement of the trackwork to the south of the station, in preparation of the closure, enabled a ne
spur to be installed from the Sheffield route and the line to Court House was severed over the Easter weekend. *David Dalton.*

The Manchester-Sheffield-Wath electrification revolutionised the haulage of mineral traffic over the Woodhead route from Yorkshire into Lancashire. A vast amount of money was expended on the creation of the scheme which included boring a new 3-mile long tunnel beneath the Pennines from Woodhead to Dunford Bridge. Some fifty-eight Bo-Bo EM1 class electric locomotives were constructed to haul the freight trains whilst seven Co-Co EM2 class locomotives were supplied to handle the passenger traffic alongside a handful of the EM1s. In this undated view from circa 1955, EM1 No.26043 has a trailing load of approximately 450-500 tons as it climbs away from Penistone at Thurlstone en route to Mottram. The view is of a typical Yorkshire Pennine landscape with rolling hills, rock outcrops, and miles of dry stone walling surrounding fields. *Unknown photographer.*

Barnsley based C13 No.67409 has charge of a Penistone-Doncaster via Barnsley passenger train on Saturday 3rd July 1954. Allocated Barnsley since January 1944, the 4-4-2T was on its fourth stint at that shed since 1935. However, this was its final period and indeed final shed as the C13 was withdrawn in December 1956 with diesel multiple units displacing steam power on many of the local passeng services in the West Riding. *K.R.Pirt.*

Mexborough based O4/3 No.63753 approaches Wath yard from the south with a heavy mineral train on 17th July 1955 – a Sunday. By now Wath had become a sort of western boundary for steam locomotion hauling coal for the still hungry industrial and domestic fires of Lancashire and Cheshire. From now on, the coal trains leaving this yard for the west were in the charge of the recently commissioned electric locomotives of EM1 class. In the background the gloom of the coal refining process at the Manvers Coking plant reminds us where indeed we are – western Yorkshire – with green fields and rolling hills on one hand, highly toxic and lucrative industrial concerns on the other, the latter courtesy of the tens of millions of tons of coal which was extracted from beneath this county annually. *Ron Hodge.*

The daily processions of coal trains arriving and departing from Wath are now simply part of Yorkshire railway history. However, in July 1955 the place couldn't handle enough coal traffic as demand throughout the country reached record levels and production reached record output. This is the same O4 as shown in the previous illustration with the train still heading north, perhaps headed for a destination other than Wath yard. Besides the train illustrated, Ron Hodge noted other loaded and empty mineral train movements taking place that Sunday which incidentally was shortly after the ASLEF dispute! *Ron Hodge.*

EM1 No.26033 runs through platform 4 at Sheffield Victoria on the morning of 16th August 1955 with eastbound mineral empties. The more usual route for the coal traffic on the MSW electric lines was via Wath yard, Worsborough and Penistone where the main line between Sheffield and Manchester was gained. However, a number of coal trains worked through to Sheffield to reach the coalfields of South Yorkshire, North Derbyshire and North Nottinghamshire. The Bo-Bo would work this train of empties to Rotherwood yard from where the wagons would be taken to the relevant collieries or washeries for filling and eventual return to the Lancashire and north Cheshire conurbation. Note that the platform canopy roof on the Up platform is covered in corrugated iron whilst the original cast iron columns supporting the structure are still in situ on both Up and Down platforms. Passenger traffic using this station was still quite brisk at this time. Besides the basic hourly service between Victoria and Manchester (London Road), there was also the through cross-country trains from Liverpool (Central) via Manchester (Central) and Guide Bridge to Hull. Besides those, the daily return working from Harwich (Parkeston Quay) to Liverpool (Central) brought East Anglian motive power in the shape of Gresley B17s and latterly 'Britannia' Pacifics. Then we had the service to the capital (Marylebone station at this time) which was the preserve of the former Great Central route and which would bring A3s, and V2s to Sheffield with such trains as the *MASTER CUTLER* and *SOUTH YORKSHIREMAN*. The former named train was eventually 'upgraded' to all Pullman stock and was diesel hauled to King's Cross from 1958 whilst the latter train, which originated in Bradford and took a tortuous route from there to reach Sheffield Vic., continued to work over the GC main line until closure and was worked in the main by Stanier Class 5s, or Thompson B1s from circa 1960 onwards. *Transport Treasury.*

The great bulk of EM2 No.27004 is evident from this undated view of the yet to be named Co-Co reversing onto a westbound passenge[r]

54 working at Victoria in 1956. *Photographer unknown.*

Two engines await their trains at Sheffield (Victoria) on the last day of June 1959. Retford B1 No.61208 is waiting for an electrically hauled Manchester (London Road)-Cleethorpes express whilst the unidentified but assuredly Leicester based V2 behind, with headboard in place, was to be the train engine for the southbound working of *THE SOUTH YORKSHIREMAN*. The station ticks over at a leisurely pace, its future assured as far as everyone – staff, customers, and enthusiasts included – were concerned. Note the transition between the old and new roofing/platform canopies. *David Dalton.*

The Victoria station pilot on 10th June 1957 was D11 'Director' No.62666 ZEEBRUGGE. Relegated to these sorts of duties by thi date, besides spending long periods in store, the D11s had all but finished their working lives and were only serving the motive powe department because they still had 'some useful work left in them'. *David Dalton.*

Brush Type 2 D5680, delivered to Darnall depot on 22nd December 1960, was the first of a batch of fourteen (D5680-D5693) new A1A-A1A diesel locomotives destined to become the standard motive power in the Sheffield district for some years to come. D5680 wasn't the first of its class to be allocated to Darnall; that distinction fell to D5671 which arrived at 41A on the previous 13th October but left Sheffield in January 1961 for Finsbury Park. From June 1961 until August 1962 a steady stream of new Brush locomotives (D5804-D5852) arrived at Darnall to give the depot the largest allocation of this successful class in the country. Even more (D5857-D5862) followed during September and October 1962, when the final member of the class were delivered to BR. This view, captured at the west end of Victoria Station shows the resplendent locomotive, complete with 41A shedplate, shortly after its debut in Sheffield. *Unknown Photographer.*

This, apparently, is 'Britannia' Pacific No.70000, without nameplates but otherwise intact being, hauled through Sheffield (Victoria) b[...]
EM1 No.26015 in June 1966. The destination of the steam locomotive is unknown – Stratford has been muted – but storage was certainl[...]
'on the cards' prior to preservation. Note the firemens' spectacle is broken! Just a half dozen years previously, this particular locomotiv[...]
along with its East Anglian based sisters, were regular, daily, visitors to this station when they arrived with the Harwich-Liverpool boa[...]
train working just after midday. After uncoupling and retiring to Darnall shed for coal, water and turning, the 'Brit' returned home vi[...]
the same route hauling the Liverpool-Harwich boat train; quite an intensive day for the Pacific involved but it wasn't finished when it go[...]
back to Parkeston because another duty then took it down to London almost immediately during the night prior to retiring to its hom[...]
shed at Stratford. *Unknown photographer.*

Before the 'Britannia's' took over the Harwich (Parkeston Quay)–Liverpool (Central) boat train workings, the train was regularly hauled for many years by Gresley B17s. During its last year of operation before being condemned in November, March based B17 No.61621 has just been released from the boat train and is seen east of Victoria station making its way to Darnall shed in July 1958. *K.R.Pirt.*

H&SE personnel look away now! On Saturday 25th October 1958, J11 No.64329 pauses for a drink whilst working the carriage pilot job at Victoria station. Having just propelled the six Pullman cars of *THE MASTER CUTLER* stock out of the station after their overnight sojourn, the 0-6-0 is taking the train for a wash and clean prior to Monday's first Up service to King's Cross. The proximity of the overhead wiring to the J11's fireman does not appear to bother either him of the driver controlling the flow of water. It might have been just 1500 volt d.c. flowing through those wires but contact would probably prove fatal. The introduction of the highly lethal 25kV overhead system eventually put paid to anyone climbing above footplate level 'under the wires' but in 1958 it was just a matter of being careful! *K.R.Pirt.*

THE MASTER CUTLER Pullman set on Saturday 25th October 1958 stabled in their weekend location at Woodburn Road carriage sidings. During the week, after their late night arrival from King's Cross, they were left in the platform at Victoria station where they were cleaned and serviced ready for early departure to London next morning. The train did two return workings each weekday, the second of which saw a 3.20 p.m. departure from Sheffield to London. The set was made up of six vehicles as follows: Brake 2nd No.70 – nearest; Kitchen 2nd No.303; Kitchen 1st Rosamund; Kitchen 1st Sappho; Kitchen 1st Plato; Brake 2nd No.68. To say that the formation was immaculate would be an understatement; all six cars were hand washed inside the station! Note the different bogies employed. *K.R.Pirt.*

Another cross-country main line train with Sheffield on its itinerary was the Bournemouth–York. Here, in August 1959, the northbound service, consisting the Southern Region green stock today (set 426), rounds the curve as it departs Sheffield (Victoria) and heads of to York behind Thompson B1 No.61066. The southbound formation would have been made up from BR(NER) maroon stock; a join venture indeed between the two regions. *K.R.Pirt.*

ound for Sheffield (Victoria) station, a deplorable looking D11 'Director' No.62660 BUTLER HENDERSON heads a Down parcels train
st Nunnery Single Line Junction signal box in August 1959. *K.R.Pirt.*

As No.62660 slowly recedes towards Victoria station with its parcels train, note the newly painted brake van, an Up express comes rour the curve with a filthy K3 No.61938 double-heading an unidentified but equally dirty V2. Such Gresley combinations were rare, especia on the ex-GC lines. The Darnall based K3 went into Doncaster works shortly after this scene was recorded; perhaps that smokebox do got too distorted to form a seal! *K.R.Pirt.*

the east of Sheffield where the Midland's 'Old road' ran to Rotherham from Chesterfield without touching Sheffield, much of the eight over that route and the adjacent ex-GCR line by-passed Sheffield. Here at Beighton on the evening of Friday 25th August 1954, O4 o.63648 heads south along the GC with a coal train for Annesley yard. *K.R.Pirt.*

Holbeck 'Crab' No.42771 runs through Beighton over the 'Old road' with a fitted freight on 25th August 1954. *K.R.Pirt.*

pparently, the J11 0-6-0s were something of a rarity on the Sheffield (Midland)–Barnsley (Court House) passenger service so this
lustration of J11 No.64452 in charge of such a working, in March 1958, is worth inclusion on that fact alone. The Barnsley based 0-6-0
 heading north through the cutting at Nunnery Main Line Junction, the line to the higher elevation at Nunnery Single Line Junction
 hidden behind the signal box and the rock formation forming the left (Up) side of the cutting. A somewhat gloomy location this but
evertheless steeped in railway history and interest. Today, this stretch of railway is as busy as ever and will hopefully remain so. *K.R.Pirt.*

Bristol based 'Jubilee' No.45651 SHOVELL takes water at Sheffield (Midland) prior to setting off for home with a west of England trai in 1956. *K.R.Pirt.*

arnsley's C14 No.67445 stables in the centre roads at Sheffield (Midland) with the empty stock for the next local stopping service to
arnsley in January 1958. Beyond, on the Down side, Ivatt Cl.2 No.41245 shunts parcels stock in a somewhat wintry scene. Few passengers
ppear to have ventured this far up the platform and probably took to the waiting rooms instead. *K.R.Pirt.*

Approaching Heeley, about a mile south of Midland station, Millhouses Stanier Class 5 No.45056 makes a rousing start as it heads an U express away from Sheffield after a slight snow fall in March 1958. *K.R.Pirt.*

The crew of Trafford Park based Fowler Class 4 tank No.42423 prepare to go off duty after servicing and turning the engine ready for its p back to Manchester (Central) with a stopping passenger train later in the day. The date is 27th March 1955, a Sunday morning to be act, with plenty of engines on shed. Behind the 2-6-4T is 'Jubilee' No.45699 GALATEA, another visitor but from further afield, Bristol rrow Road being its home shed. *K.R.Pirt.*

Old and young at Millhouses, 7th March 1954. Spring is in the air as the trees start to bud and the sun was shining brightly on this Sun[e] morning. The 1P 0-4-4T was a relative newcomer to the Sheffield depot having transferred from Burton in the previous October. It was to stay a year because in September 1954 it moved south to Nottingham but only temporarily as it was destined to spend its last year[s] traffic allocated to Retford shed from where it worked the Southwell branch alongside sisters Nos.58065 and 58085. Ivatt Cl.2 No.412[?] sporting a suitable coating of grime, was one a trio of 2-6-2Ts allocated to Millhouses at this time. *K.R.Pirt.*